TO ELEANOR

ENJOY

Patrick
Aguilar

Patag

Hearts & MINDS

BY
PATAG

authorHOUSE®

AuthorHouse™ UK Ltd.
500 Avebury Boulevard
Central Milton Keynes, MK9 2BE
www.authorhouse.co.uk
Phone: 08001974150

First published by AuthorHouse   9/4/2008

ISBN: 978-1-4343-8646-5 (sc)

Printed in the United States of America
Bloomington, Indiana

This book is printed on acid-free paper.

Table of Contents

INSIGHT • 1

POEM • 2

WORSE OFF • 3

DEAR DEMONS • 4

POETRY • 5

PRETTY FACE • 6

YOU COMPLETE ME • 7

IS SHE? • 8

LION • 10

LEAVING • 11

ROAD RAGE • 12

TOO LATE • 13

MY GIRLS • 14

SLEEP • 15

FOR MARIE • 16

GRACE • 17

HOME • 18

TEARS WITHIN • 19

CELINE AGAIN • 20

MY • 21

CELINE • 22

ENILEC • 23

FICTION • 24

ITS ALL ABOUT ME • 25

TOOTHACHE • 26

I CANT LET GO • 27

ME? • 28

INSPIRATION • 29

MY LIFES SHELF • 31

GOOD FOR • 32

HIDE • 33

GOODBYE • 34

EQUINUS-A-UM • 36

WITHIN ME • 37

GOLD LABRADOR • 38

BORN • 40

DANIEL • 41

QUIT • 42

CHANGE • 43

SAIL AWAY • 44

YOUNIS • 45

FREDDIE • 46

ILL MAKE LOVE TO YOU • 47

MUM • 48

THE EVIL INSIDE • 49

THREE-THREE-08 • 50

SALLY OMAR • 51

DON'T • 52

THE PAST IS GONE • 53

MARIE • 54

I HATE YOU!! • 55

FORGET ABOUT ME • 56

? • 57

WORDS • 58

SORRY • 59

IT'S TRUE • 60

ASH MOUNTAIN • 61

FOR YOU / THE FIRST CRY • 62

F.J.H • 63

IVE MISSED MY DEATH!! • 64

NATALIE • 65

EMILY • 67

ELIMENTS • 68

MY EMILY • 69

INSIGHT

That's the way it is!
When things change..... Can they
return to the way they were?
Can you improve on the flaws you have
And strive to get as close to perfect as is possible?
Nothing in life is or can be perfect.
But if you try with all that you possess as an individual,
You can get pretty damn close!

Patag 2008

POEM

Poem....When I'm angry,

It calms me down....

When my mind is fazed,

They break the cloud.

But what pleases me is to read aloud....

The odes I've written,

The stories I tell, about the way I feel,

The distance I fell.

WORSE OFF

When you are sad, lonely and feeling blue,

When you feel forgotten, no one loves you.....

Try to smile, lift your spirits high,

There's plenty out there, just walking by....

Don't stay alone, don't weep, don't cry....

Because you may feel sad, you may be blue,

But there's always someone.....

Worse off than you!

DEAR DEMONS

Dear demons….leave me alone!

I'm not ready….

To go home.

Your idea of what this is….

Is not my idea of what is bliss.

As the white swans glide across the lake,

How much of me can you take?

I've given all I have to give.

But now allow Patag to live,

For now I'm happy, for now I'm fine….

Don't take me yet, I need more time….

POETRY

Poetry is not just rhyme,

Poetry is not just words.

Poetry is more than that,

It's like opening a window to your soul,

Allowing the world to see....

Letting people into your heart,

Telling them your thoughts,

Explaining with words your pain or your happiness.

It's like a song you've heard or a story you've read,

Just like the songwriters and the authors.

If you can put something out there that

touches the soul of another person,

That helps to ignite the imagination

of someone that sees it....

Then why oh why keep it hidden?

Set it free! After all....Life is an eternal poem.

Share yours....

PRETTY FACE

She's not just a pretty face.
Educated,
Elegant,
Filled with grace.

She's not just a pretty girl.
Walks tall,
Head high,
Glides with a twirl.

She's not just a pretty woman.
Laughs when happy,
Cries when sad,
Speaks her opinion,
What's on her mind.

Look at that lady,
Then close your eyes,
Think of her warmth,
Let your spirits rise.

YOU COMPLETE ME

Its cold in here, hold me tight.
In your arms, in the moonlight.
Together at last, like in the past.
But let us not dwell, we knew so well,
The mistakes I made, the hurt I caused.
You need me, lets end this war,
Let's return to how it was.
No longer a rebel without a cause,
I have a target, I have a goal.
Embrace me now and make me whole.

IS SHE?

From the beginning of time,
With Adam and the apple tree....
Everything is she!

The first ever time you opened your eyes,
Looked up and smiled happily....
Everything is she!

The little girl in the playground,
Giggling with her friends,
Knowing that is where you want to be....
Everything is she!

The young girl on the subway,
With a warm smile,
Looking into her eyes wondering what you could see....
Everything is she!

The lady in the aisle of the grocery store,
Selecting carefully her evening fare,
At her table you wish to be....
Everything is she!

Visiting your mother for Sunday lunch,
Catching up on the days gone past,
The stories she tells, of when you were three....
Everything is she!

Your eight year old daughter returns home from school,
Speaks about her day,
The friends with whom she likes to play,
When she grows up, who she wants to be....
Everything is she!

All the women ever to bless your life,
Your mother, your kids, a lover, your wife.
Without these women, we could not be....
For EVERYTHING is she!!!!

LION

His eyes so deep,

A glaring stare,

Slept with one eye open.

Was always aware,

Of the world around him,

If he heard a stir,

He would growl and let out an almighty roar,

As if to speak....

I want to sleep!

Disturb me again and I will eat!

LEAVING

I'm leaving- thought I was strong.
I'm leaving- I can't go on.
I'm leaving- nothing more to give.
I'm leaving- wanting you to live.
I'm leaving- knowing I was wrong.
I'm leaving- where do I belong?
I'm leaving- for pastures new.
I'm leaving- all you said was true.
I'm leaving- I let you down.
I'm leaving- don't need me around.
I'm leaving- to get it right.
I'm leaving- going out of sight.

I'll come back- another day.
I'll come back- and you'll hear me say.
I'll come back- I'm stronger now.
I'll come back- to renew my vows.
I'll come back- mistakes no more.
I'll come back- better than before.
I'll come back- a different me.
I'll come back- you wait and see.
For now I've left, for now I'm gone,
But I will be back and I will be strong.

ROAD RAGE

Today,

I killed a man.

Invaded my space,

Glaring eyes burning into my face.

He raised a hand, all because I got close.

Scratched my car, he hit a post.

Screaming, spitting, was filled with rage.

I cowered, I'm small, didn't want to engage.

"Sorry" I said, tried to calm him down,

Grabbed my collar, he did,

Threw me to the ground.

One kick, then two, what do I do?

Rolled over, got up and my fist just flew,

One punch it was, on the bridge of his nose,

His eyes went up, me I just froze.

Sirens were blaring, still could not move,

"I'm sorry, I'm sorry," I began to cry.

"Don't take me in, I don't want to fry."

"Too late!" Said the sergeant,

"Don't you see? A crime has been done.

You'll never be free"...

TOO LATE

Flightless bird of Babylon,

I feel your pain,

I sing your song.

Plenty I have cried for you.

I was blind, I wish I knew,

Now I see what now is lost.

It is too late, I count the cost.

"Too late" you said,

Too late I feel,

Too late for us,

Too late for real.

And now that all is said and done,

Separate ways,

But it was fun....

"FUN" you said "WAS ALL IT WAS?"

If that's the case, then just "F*** OFF!".

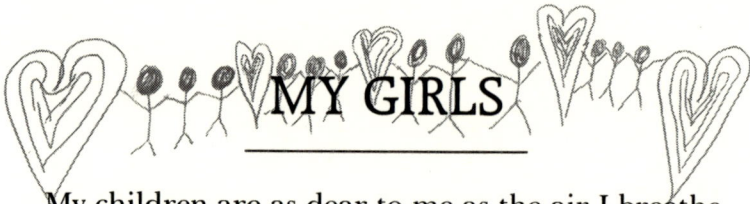

MY GIRLS

My children are as dear to me as the air I breathe,

By me leaving…. I have caused them pain…..

Through my weaknesses my children have suffered….

Through my stupidness my girls are hurting.

This has never been my wish,

This is never something I have wanted or meant to do,

But clearly it is something that I myself have done

and I myself will see things put right……..

improved………

Bettered perhaps.

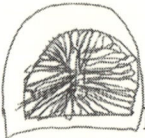

I don't want my girls to grow up hating or

have no contact with their daddy.

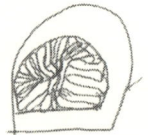

I want them to know daddy will always be there for them,

Whatever may be? Xxxxx

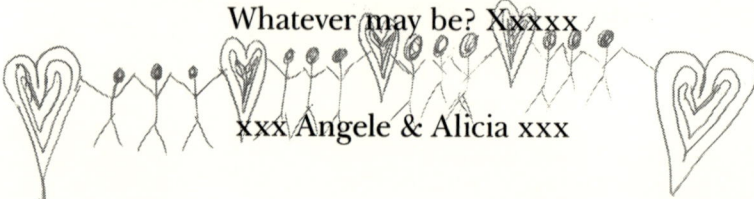

xxx Angele & Alicia xxx

SLEEP

Sleep little darling......
The world is calm,
Drift into your paradise.....
Your warm shining sun.

You're at peace now my love.....
I'll not see you again,
But in my mind always you'll be...
In my heart you'll remain.

FOR MARIE

I'll never forget the hurt i've caused....
the pain that brought your tears.

the distance that i tried to force....
will stay with me for years.

i realise now the wrong i've done....
again, it comes too late.

the feeling of you within my arms....
i've lost your loving trait.

your warmth for me has been and gone....
again i pushed too far.

you don't need me to tell you now....
how wonderful you are.

GRACE

Across the fields,
The sea of green,
The peak of the hill....
To set the scene.

The birds they sing a sound so sweet,
As if to dance on their two feet.

A day, a dawn, the rising sun,
A whole new venture just begun,
Two not one that can't be fun!

A warm embrace, your smiling face,
Her eyes so deep....
Your saving grace

HOME

I see too much,

Don't speak enough,

I want you near,

But pushed too far.....

The distance of a shining star......

You are to me and me to you,

The beating heart to see us through.

Together we can tame the beast,

Or push to one side.......

For now at least.

Don't give up and try alone.....

Allow your love...

To come back home.

TEARS WITHIN

I lie alone in my bed at night,

I cry to myself with all my might,

For what now is lost....

Can it be found?

I cry silently as not to make a sound.

I awake in the morning light,

My eyes are swollen...

From crying last night.

I pace outside in the morning dew,

cos my mind,

My thoughts....

Are only of you.

CELINE AGAIN

I sit here in my own silence,
I summarize my day.
I think of all the things I've done...
And maybe shouldn't say.

You pushed me hard,
The will is gone,
My force has well been spent.

But when I think about your smile...
You're still my heaven sent.

MY

You are my light,

My night,

My sea,

My stars....

I am nothing unless I'm in your arms.

CELINE

Warm and passionate….. You are to me.

Sexy and content….. You make me feel.

In your arms…. I long to be.

Caressing your body…. While your holding me.

Kissing your neck and holding you tight,

Till the moonlight fades….

And the sun shines bright.

ENILEC

What does it mean?
This strange short word,
It's got you thinking…. Have I heard…?
That word before?
Sounds odd to me,
Reverse the letters and you will see.

Tis for my love….
My one and only,
Tis for my heart….
Inside of me.

Of which without….
I could not exist,
To breathe the air,
To feel the cold….
To love one another….
Until were old.

FICTION

Fictions not what life's about?

But still we dream....

It all works out.

I ask you now to dream of me,

I ask you now smile happily....

Cos these two things ill do for you,

That's not fiction....

That there's the truth.

ITS ALL ABOUT ME

Let me explain my clouded mind....

So we can find....

Our direction in life,

The reason for being,

The reason for loving,

The reason for seeing.

Kiss my eyes....

For that is love,

But ask yourself.... Is love enough?

A question I have asked myself,

A feeling that can cause distress.

Embrace your sensitivity,

Forget about society,

Allow your thoughts to soar up high,

Appreciate the times gone by.

Hold and kiss those close to you,

I feel that's love,

I think that's true.

But who am I to tell you this?

My life aint great....

My life's a mess.

TOOTHACHE

God I'm in pain, my aching mouth....
What can I do?
Take it out!

Easier said than done,
You see the dentist aint cheap....
Certainly not free.

I guess I'll have to grin and bear,
Until the pains no longer there
Until my cheque is in my hand....
Then make the call....
And make a plan,

Remove the tooth,
Let me be,
Take away my pain....
And set me free.

I CANT LET GO

I can't let go….

I can't let go….

I want you back….

You need to know!

Its how I feel,

The feeling inside….

Within me is….

A love I can't hide.

I can't let go….

I can't let go.

ME?

Is it a result of me….

Or just destiny?

Was it the path I took….

Did I not look?

Could I not see?

Was it just me?

<u>YOU!</u>

You can put the blame on me….

But you know it takes two.

You can put the blame on me….

But we know it was you!

INSPIRATION

Watching the people as they pass,
Gazing at a crack in your broken glass,
Waiting for the words to form in your mind,
Seeking inspiration....
That you can't find.

Look up to the heavens,
For maybe it's there,
The world is full of people....
For whom do they care?

A mother passes your window,
With her pushchair,
Inside her baby crying,
For him she does care.

The man at the station....
What is his destination?
His job,
His love?
What gives him inspiration?

I think and I sit,
I write as they form....
The words within my mind....
To complete my poem.

To me they come one by one,
The end is nigh,
I sit,
I sigh,
I feel a deep appreciation,
For now I have my inspiration.

MY LIFES SHELF

Forgive me for what I am about to write,
My life's in a mess....
For I have no wife.

Treated her bad,
Took advantage of her love,
"Get out" she said,
"I've had enough".

Now here I am taking stock of myself,
Now here I am alone on life's shelf,
What do you do....
I hear you say,
Why did she treat you in this way?

The answer lies deep within,
Embedded well beneath my skin.

Tis I the problem,
I have to say,
Tis I the one....
Who forced her away.

Will she return?
I want to see,
Can she forgive....
And again love me?

GOOD FOR

I haven't felt for sometime….

Myself….

My inner soul.

I haven't told you how I feel….

Alone….

Not in control.

I spent too much,

Not paid enough!

Our views were not the same.

But now I see that you were right….

Betting's a mugs game,

Crying out for some attention….

I went into the wrong direction,

Till I hit the floor.

Now I sit alone and lonely….

Saying "what am I good for?"

HIDE

Darkness descends....
The days at an end.

White swans glide....
Across the pitch black lake.

Shadows emerge....
With an energy surge.

Against the building....
Under a car....
Around the corner....
They know where you are!

GOODBYE

I saw you from across the street,

The look in your eyes....

I knew we should meet.

I say hello,

You smile,

I know....

The one for me....

You are I feel,

An instant connection....

A kiss to seal?,

A growing appreciation....

A yearning temptation.

I thought unrepented passion....

Was long out of fashion,

I don't even know you....

But feel a connection,

Cross the road....

Come in my direction.

Arm in arm or hand in hand,

Our lives together....

Could be grand.

A home by the sea....

Our children's glee....

As we show them the beautiful Christmas tree.

Or maybe I'm trying to move too fast,

Let's be honest....

Does love last?

Close my eyes and think,

I try....

Should I say hello....

Or simply say goodbye?

EQUINUS-A-UM

A shiny coat of brown or grey,

I can't speak…. Just simply neigh,

An easy life I lead you see….

To run in the fields,

Like a vast green sea.

Tis what I love,

I feel so free,

Hop on my back…. and you too can see.

Now my work is done today,

I head back home….

To my bale of hay,

Ill trot, Ill sneezes,

I'll sleep on my knees.

I'll wake,

I'll take…. tomorrow with ease.

I enjoy my life,

No stress,

No strife,

Only love,

No hate,

How can this….

Not be great?

WITHIN ME

Don't let me have the choice to take….

I'll only make the same mistake,

If you could only feel my grief….

Of what I've lost beyond belief.

For what I have inside for you….

My beating heart….

A warming glow.

I feel I've lost,

No prize,

Just sin.

I take my life….

Through death I win.

GOLD LABRADOR

You are so happy and you make me laugh,

Tail swishing, tongue lashing....

You talk with your bark.

A coat so golden like the shining sun,

Not a care in the world....

You're just having fun.

Chewing my slippers,

Anything you can find,

Digging holes in the garden....

Going out of my mind.

The 25th day....

Second month of the year,

You were only ten years young,

To my eye comes a tear.

I remember the days….

Twas very funny….

Barking and running….

Playing with bunny.

I love you my baby…. I miss you so,

Oh why did the disc in your back have to go?

I cry as I write this….

I sob as before….

I miss you my Data….

My gold Labrador.

BORN

I wonder what you'll look like....
The day that you are born,
Be a boy or be a girl....
I can't wait it takes so long,
I was late before....
Three times in fact,
Again I'm overdue,
But what is sure,
I love them so....
Just as much as ill love you.

DANIEL

So far away…. You are from me,
London is such…. A big city,
Hold mummy's hand…. Don't get lost,
I could not lose you further…. And at such cost.

I'm coming soon…. To see you son,
I'll take you out…. Well have such fun.

I love you Dan…. A great deal,
My words cannot….
Describe the way I feel.

QUIT

I am ready to quit,

I can't do it,

I tried to change…. But change was strange.

The comfy armchair…. Been and gone,

Things I did…. That were so wrong.

Tried my best…. I have to say,

A new direction…. I moved away,

My problems seemed to follow me….

"Go away, let me be free"

"I want to change, I want to quit….

But whatever I try….

I can't do it!"

CHANGE

Don't know what to do anymore,

I'm not me....

I mean the me from before.

Used to be happy,

Now I am sad,

Did good things....

Now just bad.

Got to pick myself up,

Stop feeling down,

Return to before....

Not lay on the floor.

Get rid of my frown,

Move on.... On my own.

I know all this....

I know the score....

When your life is done....

There is no encore.

SAIL AWAY

Seagulls... doves...whale....dolphins....
Sail away... leave behind your sins,
Crisp blue water, bright golden sun....
Your vessel is your home now.... A new journey begun.

The ripples of the water splash against your ship....
Wind so fresh... hits your sails like a whip,
You at the helm, in control of yourself,
Controlling your destiny.... To new found wealth.

No sole you see...On the clear blue sea,
No-one to upset.... Your tranquility,
Calm and relaxed, at peace, unperplexed,
No one can annoy.... No reason to vex.

Then it hits you.... Alls not what it may seem,
Like the wind hits your sails.... Twas all but a dream,
You awake in the morn.... Eyes glazed with sleep,
Realization sets in.... turn to your pillow and weep.

YOUNIS

He is a strange one....

With long, wavy hair,

Laid back and relaxed.... As if he don't care.

Smokes a joint.... As if it weren't there....

Yet he drinks alcohol free beer.

Listens to rap.... Don't like nothing more,

Sits alone in his room.... Awaiting his next score.

Works slow.... Thinks even slower,

Can a man so tall.... Sink any lower?

Pull your finger out my friend,

Before your life reaches its end.

Life's too short.... I'm sure you've heard!

It's not about winning.... Or coming third,

It's about competing....playing the game,

Everyone is different.... Never two the same.

A friend of mine died.... His life cut short,

Leave alone the drugs...tis life you should snort

FREDDIE

Freddie plays polo....
Freddie likes sheep....
Freddie rears animals....
Every day of the week.

No rest for Freddie,
She's always ago,
There's something about Freddie....
I think you should know!

I'll tell you her story, if I may....
Good old Freddie.... Likes a roll in the hay.
Wearing her jodhpurs.... Cracking her whip,
What I wouldn't give.... To take me a sip!

She rides out her horses....
Tends to her sheep,
Invite me to your bed.... Would not be for sleep!

Her apple shaped rear.... Her rough firm hands,
Oh yes little Freddie....
For you I have plans.

ILL MAKE LOVE TO YOU

Bring me close to you.... Whisper something sweet,
Guide my hands around your body....
I'll make your knees go weak,
Groan when I touch you.... Moan when I don't,
Quiver when I touch you.... Shiver as my lips move.

We can go fast.... Or we can stay slow,
All the while we close our eyes.... We drift into our paradise,
Our bodies remain intertwined,
We gasp for air.... That we can't find,
My pulsating heart.... Beats in time with you,
You softly smile.... On your lip you chew.

The moon still shines,
We are now at ease,
Beside you my thoughts are far from deep,
As we glide into a blissful sleep.

Tomorrow is another day,
When I awake.... I'll turn and say....
"I love you girl, I love you so....
I'll hold you close.... Ill not let go!"

MUM

You cared for me…. Roye and Kenny,
We all went our separate way,
We visit you from time to time….
We dial your number to check your fine.

You are alone…. In the place you call home,
I wish that we could always be there,
I want you to know…. That we three care!
You did your best…. To raise us good,
No money you had…. For clothes or food.

Our father moved on…. He wasn't there,
When I was young…. Didn't think he cared.

My mind is fazed…. My memories poor,
Did my daddy care?…. was I wrong before?
I knew him little…. I love him still,
Feel I lost out…. Didn't get my fill.

I'm grown up now…. And times have changed,
We get more help…. Which I think is strange,
I now realize the trouble you had,
When times were hard without our dad.

I love you mum…. I mean that too,
Ill love no-one else…. As I love you.

THE EVIL INSIDE

I'm getting fed up with all of this....
I feel that now you take the piss!
At first I thought it was just a bluff,
But now I see.... You've had enough.

Told me to stop, to let it be....
To fight the evil.... Inside of me,
I didn't quit, did not take heed,
Gave in to weakness.... Succumbed to greed.

The devils horns came through my hair,
You threw me out.... Didn't want me there,
I walk the streets a lonely soul,
I need you back.... To make me whole.

Can't you see.... The evils gone,
I fought the devil.... And now I'm strong,
Again the man you loved before,
But still you seem.... As though unsure!
What will it take to make you see.....
The devil is .....No longer me?

THREE-THREE-08

Today's my birthday yet I'm here alone,
No-one to hold and call my own,
So many things going through my mind,
Yet words to describe.... I just can't find.

There was a day when all was great,
But now my heart has too much hate,
It brings me down.... I bare a frown,
The smiles gone.... This is just wrong.

What do I do?
I tell myself,
I said before I'm on life's shelf,
Can't get down.... Cannot escape,
Can't shake my frown,
Can't erase my hate.

Is it hate for me?
Or hate for her?
I feel right now....
I just don't care.

SALLY OMAR

I don't know you…. Never seen your face,
I enjoy your work…. You write at such pace.

I can't keep up…. Cannot compete,
Our styles so different…. Your comments so sweet.

I enjoy reading…. All that you do,
Your words of wisdom…. They see me through.

My life at present…. Not at its best,
Before red bubble…. Considered a rest.

Now I have focus,
Rebuild my life…. Love my children,
Forget my wife.

Because of you and your support….
I can now make…. A brand new start.

DON'T

Don't look at me like that,
Don't make me feel ashamed,
Don't cry your tears…. There not for me,
Just wipe the things away.

I see you're sad,
For this imp glad…. Redemption for my pain,
Let go of me and start again,
You're driving me insane.

Shame on me and blame on you,
Eleven years of hurt,
Yet now you smile….. Did take awhile,
Tis time I did depart.

THE PAST IS GONE

Do you ever wish.... You could go back
and change the path you took?
Do you dream.... Of what now could
be..... To take a second look?
If you could.... What would you change?
And would your future re-arrange?
Would it improve?
Or maybe not?
Should you be thankful..... For what you've got?

Would the birds sing sweeter?
Could the grass be greener?
Can the sun shine brighter?
I guess you'll never know!

The futures bleak.... The past is gone,
For now you must.... Just soldier on.

MARIE

Don't look to the left,

Look me in the eye,

Show me what you like…. Tell me what to try.

Does that feel good?

Is it better like this?

Whilst you're on top…. Reach down and kiss,

My lips are yours…. My body too,

My mind it wonders with thoughts of you.

Sweet Marie you are so kind,

Too good for me…. I think you'll find,

Let us enjoy…. What we now have,

The futures unclear…. For now I'm sincere.

I'm happy with you,

As you are with I,

Let us two be happy…. Let time drift by,

In time we'll see…. Was it just fun?

In time we'll see…. Are you the one?

I HATE YOU!!

To me you are hell,
You drive me mad.
The hate I feel…. It makes me sad,
Loved you once…. But not again,
Said I want you back…. You say let us be friends.

With these four words I hate you more,
There is someone else…. Of this I'm sure,
Well go ahead and do your deed,
Enjoy your life and please succeed.

It's what you want and who am I?
Your husband…. Your love,
Till the day I die.

FORGET ABOUT ME

Drink your cointreau – forget about me,
Take your pills – forget about me,
Live your life – forget about me,
Listen to your friends – forget about me.

When your friends are gone – remember me,
When your life is lived – remember me,
When the pills are spent – remember me,
When the spirits gone – remember me.

I made mistakes…. Well quite a few,
But what is sure…. I'll never forget you.

?

Isn't she lovely?

The girl within your dreams,

Isn't she.... Not all what she may seem?

Close your eyes and think....

Of all the things you'd like to do,

Open them.... Then look at her,

Does she want the same things too?

WORDS

When I write they just come,
The words they flow.... So I just choose some,
All around us.... Every day,
Select your words.... Before you say.

There are so many.... It's hard to find,
The sentence flying round your mind,
When you select your chosen choice.....
Write them down and share your voice.

SORRY

It's easy to say I'm sorry,

Just as easy to regret,

You say the word, you turn…. And easily forget,

Pass it off like nothing,

Although you seem sincere,

Mutter it repeatedly…. As though you really care.

Too many culprits use this word….

I have to say me too!,

Sometimes you really mean it,

In the moment it feels true.

How many times have you used it….

In your life up until now?

How many times have you meant it,

With true remorse that you can show?

The next time that you think it,

Remember what's been written,

To say such a word with emptiness….

Is easily forgotten.

IT'S TRUE

Because of you I'm now just a lonely man,
Which way to go I know.…. But don't know if I can,
As the days go by and the years extend,
Regret what I have lost.… And the time I failed to spend.

Remember me with fondness,
Forget the wrong I've done,
Was not so long ago.….. You thought I was the one.

Its true love makes us stronger!
It's true the weak die young!
It's true I loved you dearly!
Tis true I AM the one!!

ASH MOUNTAIN

Tall, slender, perfection at a glance,

Sweet yet demure.... I ask only one chance,

To climb the mountain of soft skin,

The pink velvet to let me in.

The lights go down as I rise up,

A challenging feat.... The nectar cup,

A will so strong, a belief so bold,

You smile with your eyes.... As a passion takes hold.

Let yourself go.... Allow passion to flow,

My heart pounds to the beat of yours,

One final push to reach the top,

Climb that mountain....

Push right up.

FOR YOU / THE FIRST CRY

I love you before I can see your face,

For you my unborn…. I write this piece,

For when you are born…. You'll bring us bliss.

Boy or girl…. No matter each way,

For when you are here…. We will love you each day,

When you can crawl…. With the terriers you'll play,

Don't forget Beechy…. He'll lick you all day.

Your family waits for you to arrive,

Your brother, your sisters….

George and I make five,

Thought we were complete till I fell with you.

Then heard your heart beat….

Saw your silhouette….

A sight I myself….

Will never forget.

I await the day that you are born….

The first cry…

Of my unborn.

F.J.H

Now you are here within my arms,

My gorgeous baby boy,

When you arrived....

You wailed aloud.... As I cried tears of joy.

The thoughts of all there is to come....

Excites me every day,

You are now the new green leaf....

On the tree of Hosier.

Let your guardian angel watch over you...

Be your guiding light to see you through,

Our families' strength....

Combined as one,

On the birth of my Frederick,

Our new born son.

IVE MISSED MY DEATH!!

I'm starting to think…. What is the point?
When everything you do…. Never seems to be right.
Why did I not listen…. To what was said?
Now I feel…. Inside I'm dead.

When I was born… I came with a complication,
As I grew…. Thought I knew the right direction!
Now I see what I thought was wrong,
What will it take…. To make me again strong?

What can I do to find a new you?
Someone to share…. My strange point of view!
Cannot seem to answer right now,
I lost my direction…. Although I know how.

Can I rebuild the foundations I've lost?
Can I improve to find new found wealth?
Could I stop smoking to improve my health?
Many a question said within one breath…..
What is the answer to again miss my death?

NATALIE

I am writing this to tell you….
Just how much it is I miss you,
I am thinking of you always….
Within my heart you'll be for all days,
Till the day we meet again….
My confident and one true friend.

Your smile was infectious….
Was the first thing to connect us,
You're crazy ways, you're dancing feet,
Was fate that you and I should meet.

Some days you failed to leave your house,
Sat quiet inside like a tiny mousse,
The phone would ring….you would not move….
Of this dear Nat… I did not approve.

But I understand what you went through….
When you were young… he would touch you,
No one needs to feel that way,
So brave you were each passing day.

I wish I could have done more....
I wish I could erase before,
I dream that you are still with me,
I have moved on....
Can you still see?

Your baby she is just like you,
Your eyes, your smile....
You know it's true!
She seems so happy.... And stubborn too,
But I guess that's why.... She's just like you.

Dear Nat, I miss all that you were,
The joy you gave to me before,
I'll see you soon.... Of that I'm sure.

For now please wait, watch over me....
Protect me from what I can't see,
Be now my angel.... My guiding light,
The warmth I feel...
Alone at night.

EMILY

I love you more than words can say,
my feelings grow for you each day,
to be with you is what I wish ...
to stroke your cheek and feel your kiss.

ELIMENTS

as i watch the water ripple by,
i reminisce as time flies by.

with a sky so blue and clouds so white,
i pen my thoughts with warm delight.

the spires of the church ahead,
the swaying trees above my head ...
as the wind it whistles lovingly,
as if to sing your name to me.

MY EMILY

amazing as it may seem ...
straight forward as things may be ...
my feelings for you they are so strong ...
without you i just could not go on.

a smile so sweet with lips so soft ...
as i see you, i feel a draft,
but not of cold,
i feel at last ...
i've found my heart,
my soul within,
to kiss your smooth, pink, supple skin.

the warmth within you give to me ...
i love you so ... my Emily.

Printed in the United Kingdom
by Lightning Source UK Ltd.
133320UK00002B/250-297/P